STEAM
Project-Based Learning

GRADE 1

All illustrations and photography, including those from Shutterstock.com, are protected by copyright.

Writing: Tiffany Rivera
Content Editing: Teera Robinson
Lisa Vitarisi Mathews
Copy Editing: Laurie Westrich
Cathy Harber
Art Direction: Yuki Meyer
Cover Design: Yuki Meyer
Illustration: Mary Rojas
Design/Production: Jessica Onken

EMC 3111

Evan-Moor.™

Visit
teaching-standards.com
to view a correlation
of this book.
This is a free service.

**Correlated to
Current Standards**

**Congratulations on your purchase of some of the
finest teaching materials in the world.**

For information about other Evan-Moor products, call 1-800-777-4362,
fax 1-800-777-4332, or visit our website, www.evan-moor.com.
Entire contents © 2022 Evan-Moor Corporation
18 Lower Ragsdale Drive, Monterey, CA 93940-5746. Printed in USA.

CPSIA: McNaughton & Gunn, Saline, MI USA [2/2022]

Contents

    Real-World Connection: Ocean pollution harms people, animals, and the environment.

    Art Connection: Make artwork out of recyclable items.

    Science and Math Connections: Decomposition; Sorting recyclable items

    Career Spotlight: Environmental engineers

    STEAM Task: Design and make a machine that will gather litter and help clean the community.

    Real-World Connection: Pictures can communicate important information and help people learn about a culture and its language.

    Art Connection: Make a poster with pictures that show classroom rules.

    Technology and Math Connections: Inferring picture meaning on signs; Relating geometric shapes to signs

    Career Spotlight: Comic book artists

    STEAM Task: Make a picture book that tells a story.

    Real-World Connection: Clean water is necessary for survival, but some people do not have access to clean water.

    Art Connection: Make a Native American rainstick and an African drum.

    Math and Science Connections: Bar graphs; Addition; Identify salt water and fresh water

    Career Spotlight: Jobs that help people get clean water

    STEAM Task: Make a water collector that filters water.

    Real-World Connection: Playtime is very important, but not all schools offer enough choices for different children's interests.

    Art Connection: Make a dance box that lists dance moves.

    Math and Science Connections: Counting; Subtracting; Dividing; Drawing playground exercise

    Career Spotlight: Dancers

    STEAM Task: Make a game that uses music and movement.

What's Inside

Organization of Each Unit

Each unit in *STEAM Project-Based Learning* focuses on a real-world problem and features a realistic fiction text, a nonfiction text, an art project, and a variety of activities that focus on science, technology, engineering, and math. In addition, each unit includes a career connection that features real-world jobs. Following is a description of each component of the unit and the role it plays and its value for students.

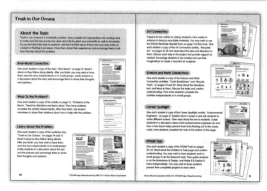

Teacher Page

Each unit begins with teacher pages that provide an overview of the unit, information about the topic, and suggestions for implementing the lesson.

Real-World Connection

Each unit begins with a Real-World Connection text that focuses on the topic through a one-page realistic fiction story. The story provides context for students to understand the problem and possibly empathize with the people or animals that this problem affects. The story often includes multiple problems connected to the topic. Some problems are First World, such as safe bike lanes and skate parks, and some are Third World, such as clean drinking water.

What Is the Problem?

The What Is the Problem? page follows the Real-World Connection story, and it focuses on having students identify one or more problems in the story. The items in this activity will help students think about the problem or problems that were presented and identify possible solutions from the story or from their own thoughts.

Learn About the Problem

Each unit includes a nonfiction text that provides students with more detailed information about the problem in the real world. Meaningful photos and illustrations provide context and enrich students' understanding of the problem.

Art Connection

Each unit includes an Art Connection activity that incorporates creativity into finding solutions. These activities provide an opportunity to be creative and to learn about how to relate topics to art and present information in an engaging way.

Science, Technology, Engineering, and Math Connections

The Science, Technology, and Engineering Connection activities present additional information about how these emphases are used to solve problems. The Math Connection activities relate the problems to a variety of real-world situations in which math concepts can be used to figure out solutions.

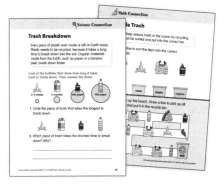

Career Spotlight

The Career Spotlight activities present a variety of careers related to the problems or solutions in the unit. These activities provide students with a real-world view of science, technology, engineering, art, and math jobs and careers.

STEAM Task

Each unit culminates with a STEAM Task. The STEAM Task gives students a real-world scenario and a problem to solve using the following design process: Problem & Task, Research, Brainstorm & Design, Make It & Explain It. Students present their completed project, product, or other creation to an authentic audience.

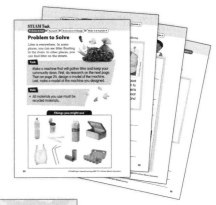

Certificate and STEAM Puzzle

This book includes a student certificate and STEAM puzzle. These reproducible bonus materials are intended to provide students with a visual reminder of their accomplishments after completing the STEAM lessons, activities, and tasks.

How to Use This Book

The information and practice in *STEAM Project-Based Learning* introduces students to real-world problems in relatable contexts. The activities and projects focus on Science, Technology, Engineering, Art, and Math and provide hands-on experiences as well as connections to real-world scenarios and careers.

There are many approaches you may take in incorporating these lessons and activities into your curriculum. It all depends on the amount of time and resources you have available to dedicate to project-based learning. Here are some suggestions:

- Do one project each month for seven months.
- Choose four units and do one unit each quarter.
- Send home units for students to do with their families.

How to Use the STEAM Approach to Education

STEAM is an approach to education that focuses on using Science, Technology, Engineering, Art, and Math to solve real-world problems. Empathy is at the core of STEAM education. Understanding how people, animals, or things are affected by a problem is an important part of the problem-solving and solution-seeking process. Teaching children how to think creatively prepares them for new unknown technologies, industries, and careers.

With STEAM activities and tasks, the final product is not as important as the process. Through the process of experimenting and exploring, your child is using creative and critical thinking skills. Scientists, mathematicians, engineers, and artists use the same critical thinking skills to find new and innovative solutions.

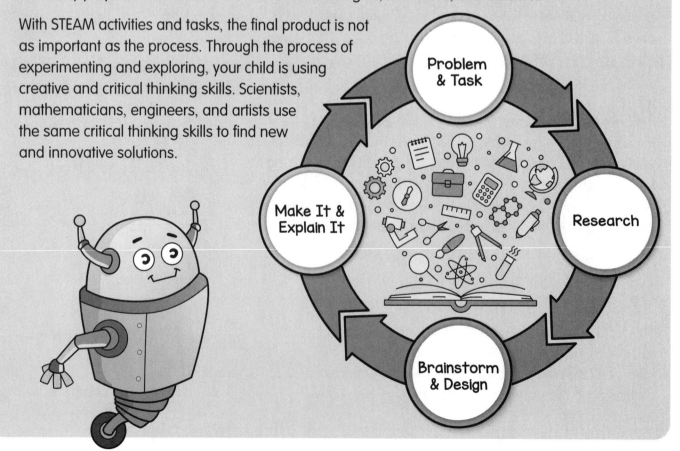

Problem & Task

Research

Brainstorm & Design

Make It & Explain It

STEAM Rubric

Name: _____

Unit: _____

	Needs Guidance	Proficient	Notes
Student understands the problem			
Student provides solutions to the problem			
Student relates the problem to his or her own life			
Student empathizes			
Student understands science concept on Science Connection page			
Student demonstrates math skills on Math Connection page			
Student identifies technological items on Technology Connection page			
Student shows creativity when completing art projects			
Student understands how the occupation highlighted on the Career Spotlight page helps with the problem			

General Materials List

- water bottle
- metal can
- craft sticks
- milk carton
- shoebox
- plastic bag
- straws
- toilet paper rolls
- egg carton
- string
- hole punch
- white paper
- colored paper
- colored markers
- tape
- aluminum foil
- Legos
- pipe cleaners
- rubber bands
- plastic cups

- plastic wrap
- aluminum tin/container
- paper plate
- paper bowl
- sponge
- rocks
- tennis ball
- boom box
- rope
- stopwatch
- hula hoop
- laundry basket
- wax paper
- ruler
- scissors
- paper cup
- colored pencils
- paint
- paper bag

STEAM Project-Based Learning • EMC 3111 • © Evan-Moor Corporation

STEAM Materials Needed

Dear Parent/Guardian,

Our class is doing a STEAM activity on ______________________.
(date)

Can you please provide the following materials by the date above?

______________________ ______________________

______________________ ______________________

Thank you!

Sincerely,

______________________, Room __________

Reproduce and distribute to students.

STEAM Materials Needed

Dear Parent/Guardian,

Our class is doing a STEAM activity on ______________________.
(date)

Can you please provide the following materials by the date above?

______________________ ______________________

______________________ ______________________

Thank you!

Sincerely,

______________________, Room __________

About the Topic

Trash in our oceans is a worldwide problem. Many people and organizations are working hard to make sure that our oceans are clean and safe for plant and animal life as well as for people. As you introduce this topic to students, ask them to think about if they have ever seen trash on a beach or floating in an ocean. Have them share their experiences and encourage them to tell how they feel about this problem.

Real-World Connection

Give each student a copy of the story "Dirty Beach" on page 12. Read it aloud as they follow along silently. After you finish, you may wish to have them read the story independently or in small groups. Guide students in a discussion about the story and encourage them to share their thoughts and opinions.

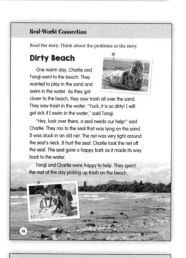

What Is the Problem?

Give each student a copy of the activity on page 13, "Problems at the Beach." Read the directions and items aloud. Then have students complete the activity independently. After they finish, ask student volunteers to share their solutions about how to help with the problem.

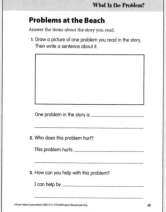

Learn About the Problem

Give each student a copy of the nonfiction text, "Trash in Our Oceans," on pages 14 and 15. Read it aloud as they follow along silently. After you finish, you may wish to have them read the text independently or in small groups. Guide students in a discussion about the text and the pictures and encourage them to share their thoughts and opinions.

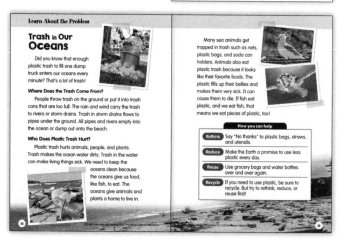

Art Connection

Prepare for the activity by asking students a few weeks in advance to bring in recyclable materials. You may wish to use the STEAM Materials Needed form on page 9 of this book. Give each student a copy of the Art Connection activity, "Recycled Art," on pages 16–18 and read aloud the text and directions to them. Discuss each step in the project and provide support as needed. Encourage students to be creative and use their imaginations to create a recycled art sculpture.

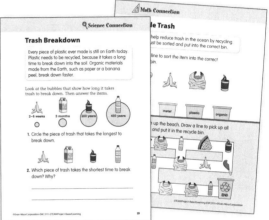

Science and Math Connections

Give each student a copy of the Science and Math Connection activities, "Trash Breakdown" and "Recycle Trash," on pages 19 and 20. Read aloud the directions, text, and items to them. Discuss the tasks and confirm understanding. Then have students complete the activities independently or in small groups.

Career Spotlight

Give each student a copy of the Career Spotlight activity, "Environmental Engineers," on page 21. Explain what a career is and ask students to name different careers. Then read aloud the text to students. Guide students in a discussion about what environmental engineers do and how a river boom helps prevent trash from floating out to the ocean. Lastly, have students complete the task at the bottom of the page.

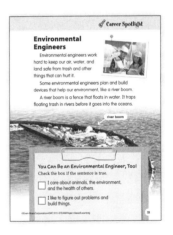

STEAM Task

Give each student a copy of the STEAM Task on pages 22–25. Read aloud the Problem & Task page and confirm understanding. You may wish to have students work in small groups to do the Research task. Then guide students to do the Brainstorm & Design and Make It & Explain It tasks independently. You may wish to have students present their completed projects to each other.

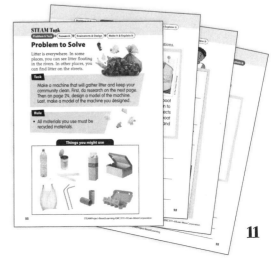

Read the story. Think about the problems in the story.

Dirty Beach

One warm day, Charlie and Taraji went to the beach. They wanted to play in the sand and swim in the water. As they got closer to the beach, they saw trash all over the sand. They saw trash in the water. "Yuck, it is so dirty! I will get sick if I swim in the water," said Taraji.

"Hey, look over there, a seal needs our help!" said Charlie. They ran to the seal that was lying on the sand. It was stuck in an old net. The net was very tight around the seal's neck. It hurt the seal. Charlie took the net off the seal. The seal gave a happy bark as it made its way back to the water.

Taraji and Charlie were happy to help. They spent the rest of the day picking up trash on the beach.

STEAM Project-Based Learning • EMC 3111 • © Evan-Moor Corporation

Problems at the Beach

Answer the items about the story you read.

1. Draw a picture of one problem you read in the story. Then write a sentence about it.

One problem in the story is _____

_____.

2. Who does this problem hurt?

This problem hurts _____

_____.

3. How can you help with this problem?

I can help by _____

_____.

Trash in Our Oceans

Did you know that enough plastic trash to fill one dump truck enters our oceans every minute? That's a lot of trash!

Where Does the Trash Come From?

People throw trash on the ground or put it into trash cans that are too full. The rain and wind carry the trash to rivers or storm drains. Trash in storm drains flows to pipes under the ground. All pipes and rivers empty into the ocean or dump out onto the beach.

Who Does Plastic Trash Hurt?

Plastic trash hurts animals, people, and plants. Trash makes the ocean water dirty. Trash in the water can make living things sick. We need to keep the

oceans clean because the oceans give us food, like fish, to eat. The oceans give animals and plants a home to live in.

Many sea animals get trapped in trash such as nets, plastic bags, and soda can holders. Animals also eat plastic trash because it looks like their favorite foods. The plastic fills up their bellies and makes them very sick. It can cause them to die. If fish eat plastic, and we eat fish, that means we eat pieces of plastic, too!

How you can help

Rethink	Say "No thanks" to plastic bags, straws, and utensils.
Reduce	Make the Earth a promise to use less plastic every day.
Reuse	Use grocery bags and water bottles over and over again.
Recycle	If you need to use plastic, be sure to recycle. But try to rethink, reduce, or reuse first!

Recycled Art

Many artists around the world have taken trash found on beaches and made it into sculptures. They help remind people how litter can pollute oceans and hurt our environment.

Make a sculpture out of recycled items.

Step 1: Brainstorm

- Think about why you are using recycled items to make art.

- What kind of sculpture can you make to help people remember to stop littering?

- How do you want people to feel when they see your sculpture?

These pictures show art made from recycled items.

Think about these questions
as you look at the pictures.

- What do you like about the art?

- What do you not like about the art?

- What items were used
  to make the art?

- How do you feel when
  you look at the art?

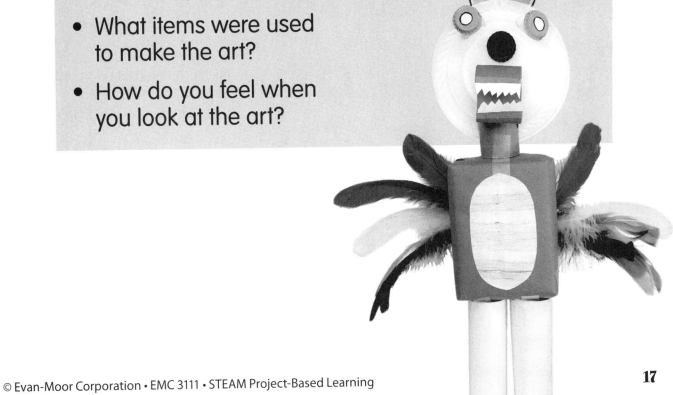

Step 3: Plan

Choose the things you want you use.
Here are some things you might want to use:

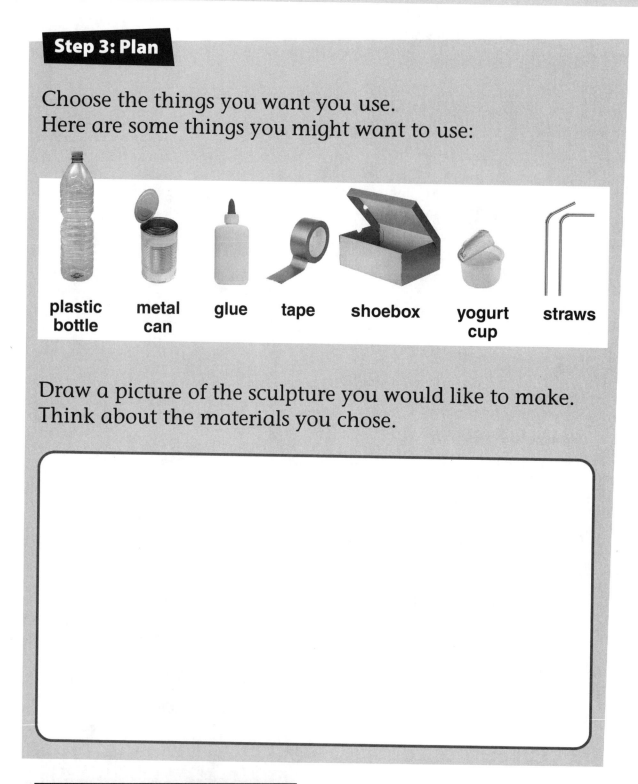

| plastic bottle | metal can | glue | tape | shoebox | yogurt cup | straws |

Draw a picture of the sculpture you would like to make.
Think about the materials you chose.

Step 4: Make It and Share It

Make your sculpture. Then show it to a friend.
Tell your friend why you made it.

Trash Breakdown

Every piece of plastic ever made is still on Earth today. Plastic needs to be recycled, because it takes a long time to break down into the soil. Organic materials made from the Earth, such as paper or a banana peel, break down faster.

Look at the bubbles that show how long it takes trash to break down. Then answer the items.

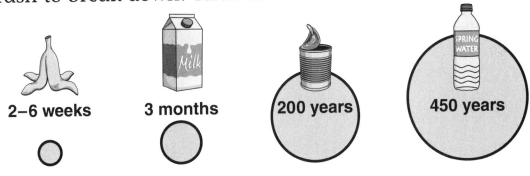

2–6 weeks   **3 months**   **200 years**   **450 years**

1. Circle the piece of trash that takes the longest to break down.

2. Which piece of trash takes the shortest time to break down? Why?

_____

_____

Recycle Trash

You can help reduce trash in the ocean by recycling. Items must be sorted and put into the correct bin.

1. Draw a line to sort the item into the correct recycle bin.

| paper | metal | plastic | organic |

2. Help clean up the beach. Draw a line to pick up all the plastic and put it in the recycle bin.

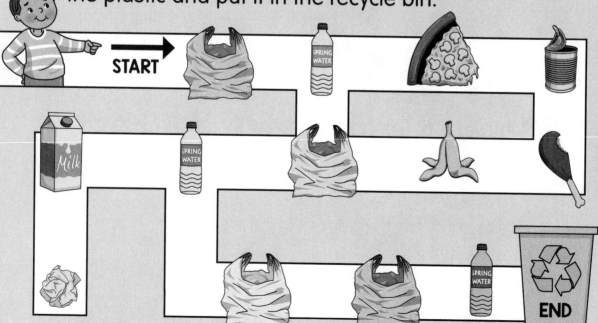

Environmental Engineers

Environmental engineers work hard to keep our air, water, and land safe from trash and other things that can hurt it.

Some environmental engineers plan and build devices that help our environment, like a river boom.

A river boom is a fence that floats in water. It traps floating trash in rivers before it goes into the oceans.

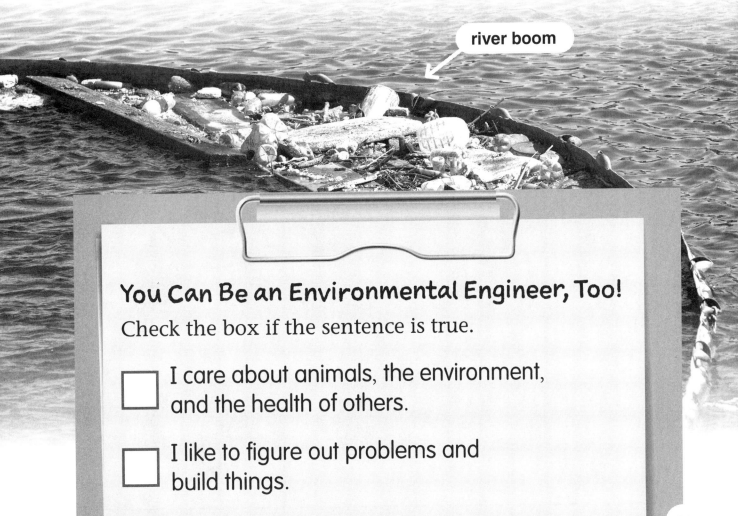

river boom

You Can Be an Environmental Engineer, Too!

Check the box if the sentence is true.

☐ I care about animals, the environment, and the health of others.

☐ I like to figure out problems and build things.

Problem to Solve

Litter is everywhere. In some places, you can see litter floating in the rivers. In other places, you can find litter on the streets.

Task

Make a machine that will gather litter and keep your community clean. First, do research on the next page. Then on page 24, design a model of the machine. Last, make a model of the machine you designed.

Rule

- All materials you use must be recycled materials.

Things you might use

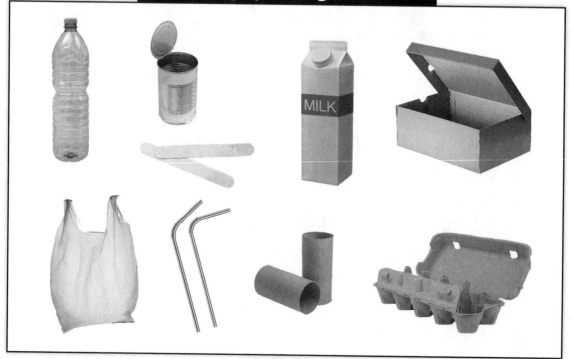

The Clean-up Boat

Read. Look at the pictures. Then answer the questions.

© The Ocean Cleanup

The Ocean Cleanup is a company that made a boat called the Interceptor. It uses power from the sun to move in rivers. A moving belt inside the boat collects floating trash and drops it into big buckets. The boat sends a text message when the buckets are full and ready to be emptied.

1. Can this machine be used on water or on land?

_____

2. How does this machine collect trash?

_____

3. What do you like most about this machine?

_____

Litter Machine Brainstorm

Answer these questions to help you brainstorm ideas for your machine.

1. Where do you see the most litter in your community?

_____

2. What would make people want to use your machine?

_____

3. Does your machine work on water, land, or both?

_____

Now draw a picture of what your machine will look like. Think about the materials you will use.

STEAM Project-Based Learning • EMC 3111 • © Evan-Moor Corporation

Make Your Litter Machine

Make a model of the machine you designed.

Then take a picture of it and glue the picture below.
Or draw a picture of your model in the box.

Finish the sentences to tell more about your machine.

My machine is called _____.

This is how it works:

_____

_____

_____

The Power of Pictures

About the Topic

Pictures are all around us. People use pictures such as photos, illustrations, and other graphic images to communicate. Pictures have meaning. This unit addresses how pictures and signs are helpful to people, especially people who are in an environment in which people speak a different language than they do. Invite students to share their experiences about how pictures and signs help them and discuss how they may be helpful to their classmates who speak a different language.

Real-World Connection

Give each student a copy of the story "New School, New Language" on page 28. Read it aloud as they follow along silently. After you finish, you may wish to have them read the story independently or in small groups. Guide students in a discussion about the story and encourage them to share their thoughts and opinions.

What Is the Problem?

Give each student a copy of the activity on page 29, "New Language Problems." Read the directions and items aloud. Then have students complete the activity independently. After they finish, ask student volunteers to share additional solutions about how pictures can help people.

Learn About the Problem

Give each student a copy of the nonfiction text, "Talking Without Words," on pages 30 and 31. Read it aloud as they follow along silently. After you finish, you may wish to have them read the text independently or in small groups. Guide students in a discussion about the text and the pictures and encourage them to share their own stories about how pictures have helped them or someone they know.

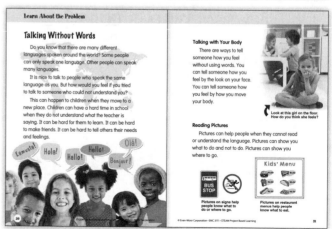

Art Connection

Give each student a copy of the Art Connection activity, "Classroom Rules," on pages 32–34 and read aloud the text and directions to them. Review the classroom rules and have students think of other things their classmates who do not read or speak the language need to know. Discuss each step in the project and provide support as needed. Remind students that even a simple picture such as a smiley face has meaning.

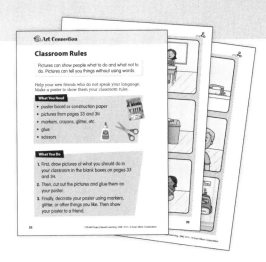

Technology and Math Connections

Give each student a copy of the Technology and Math Connection activities, "Signs That Help" and "Shapes and Signs," on pages 35 and 36. Read aloud the directions, text, and items to them. Discuss the tasks and confirm understanding. Provide support with spelling and writing words. Then have students complete the activities independently or in small groups.

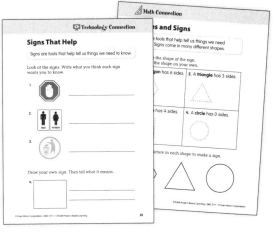

Career Spotlight

Give each student a copy of the Career Spotlight activity, "Comic Book Artists," on page 37. Explain what a career is and ask students to name different careers. Then read aloud the text to students. Guide students in a discussion about what comic book artists do. Have them tell about their favorite picture books. Lastly, have students draw pictures to finish the story.

STEAM Task

Give each student a copy of the STEAM Task on pages 38–41. Read aloud the Problem & Task page and confirm understanding. Then guide students to do the Research, Brainstorm & Design, and Make It & Explain It tasks independently. You may wish to have students present their completed books to each other.

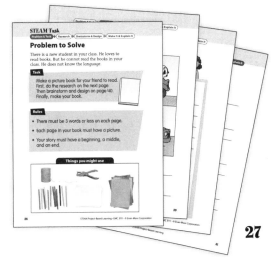

Read the story. Think about the problems in the story.

New School, New Language

"Hello, class. This is our new friend, Miguel. He moved here from Mexico. Miguel, tell the class about your family," says the teacher.

Miguel tells his new class about his family. But everyone in the class is looking at him funny. Miguel is speaking Spanish. But his classmates only speak English. They don't know what he is saying. How can Miguel help them understand him?

Miguel grabs a marker and draws a picture of his family on the board. "I see that Miguel has a mom, a dad, and a big sister," says Sally. Miguel is happy that Sally could read his picture.

Later, Miguel needs to pick up some books from the library. He also needs to use the restroom. But how can Miguel find those places?

"Look at the pictures on the signs. They show you where you are," says Sally.

Miguel finds each place at school by looking at the pictures on the signs.

New Language Problems

Answer the items about the story you read.

1. Draw a picture of one problem you read about in the story. Then finish the sentence about it.

One problem in the story is _____

_____.

2. How was the problem fixed?

This problem was fixed when _____

_____.

Talking Without Words

Do you know that there are many different languages spoken around the world? Some people can only speak one language. Other people can speak many languages.

It is nice to talk to people who speak the same language as you. But how would you feel if you tried to talk to someone who could not understand you?

This can happen to children when they move to a new place. Children can have a hard time in school when they do not understand what the teacher is saying. It can be hard for them to learn. It can be hard to make friends. It can be hard to tell others their needs and feelings.

Talking with Your Body

There are ways to tell someone how you feel without using words. You can tell someone how you feel by the look on your face. You can tell someone how you feel by how you move your body.

Look at this girl on the floor. How do you think she feels?

Reading Pictures

Pictures can help people when they cannot read or understand the language. Pictures can show you what to do and not to do. Pictures can show you where to go.

Pictures on signs help people know what to do or where to go.

Pictures on restaurant menus help people know what to eat.

Classroom Rules

Pictures can show people what to do and what not to do. Pictures can tell you things without using words.

Help your new friends who do not speak your language. Make a poster to show them your classroom rules.

What You Need

- poster board or construction paper
- pictures from pages 33 and 34
- markers, crayons, glitter, etc.
- glue
- scissors

What You Do

1. First, draw pictures of what you should do in your classroom in the blank boxes on pages 33 and 34.

2. Then, cut out the pictures and glue them on your poster.

3. Finally, decorate your poster using markers, glitter, or other things you like. Then show your poster to a friend.

Signs That Help

Signs are tools that help tell us things we need to know.

Look at the signs. Write what you think each sign wants you to know.

1.  _____

2.  _____

3.  _____

Draw your own sign. Then tell what it means.

4.  _____

_____

Shapes and Signs

> Signs are tools that help tell us things we need
> to know. Signs come in many different shapes.

Read. Trace the shape of the sign.
Then draw the shape on your own.

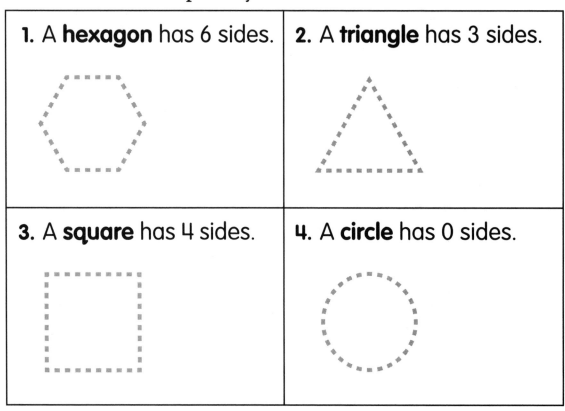

1. A **hexagon** has 6 sides.

2. A **triangle** has 3 sides.

3. A **square** has 4 sides.

4. A **circle** has 0 sides.

Now draw a picture in each shape to make a sign.

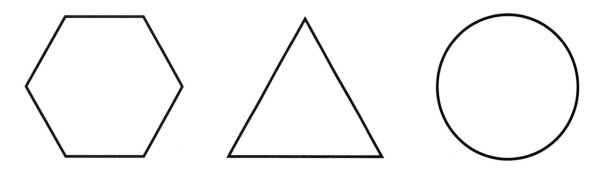

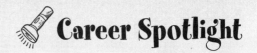
Comic Book Artists

Comic book artists are people who draw pictures to tell a story. Each part of the story is found in a different box. Sometimes comic books have pictures and words. Sometimes they have only pictures.

You can be a comic book artist, too. Finish the story by drawing pictures in the boxes.

Problem to Solve

There is a new student in your class. He loves to read books. But he cannot read the books in your class. He does not know the language.

Task

Make a picture book for your friend to read. First, do the research on the next page. Then brainstorm and design on page 40. Finally, make your book.

Rules

- There must be 3 words or less on each page.

- Each page in your book must have a picture.

- Your story must have a beginning, a middle, and an end.

Things you might use

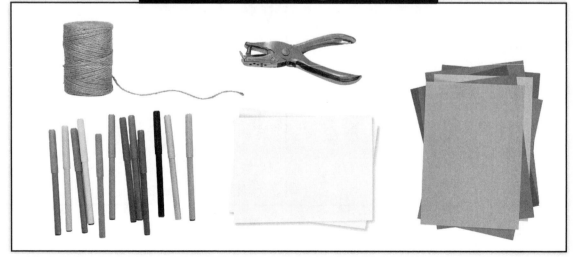

Picture Books

Look at the pictures.
Then answer the questions.

1. What happens in the story?

_____

2. How do you know?

_____

Book Brainstorm

Think about the book you want to make. Then write and draw pictures to answer the questions. They will help you brainstorm ideas for your book.

1. Where does your story happen?

_____

_____

_____

_____

2. Who is in your story?

_____

_____

_____

A Book for a Friend

Make your picture book. Next, write sentences to tell more about your book. Then give your book to a friend to read.

1. My book is called _____.

2. Write what happens in the beginning.

_____

_____.

3. Write what happens in the middle.

_____

_____.

4. Write what happens at the end.

_____

_____.

Clean Water

Real-World Connection

Give each student a copy of the story "The Walk to the Well" on page 44. Read it aloud as they follow along silently. After you finish, you may wish to have them read the story independently or in small groups. Guide students in a discussion about the story and encourage them to share their thoughts and feelings.

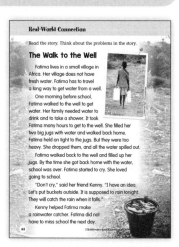

What Is the Problem?

Give each student a copy of the activity on page 45, "Problems Getting Water." Read the directions and items aloud. Then have students complete the activity independently. After they finish, ask student volunteers to share their solutions about how to help with the problem.

Learn About the Problem

Give each student a copy of the nonfiction text, "We Need Clean Water," on pages 46 and 47. Read it aloud as they follow along silently. After you finish, you may wish to have them read the text independently or in small groups. Guide students in a discussion about the text and the pictures and encourage them to share their thoughts and feelings about the problem.

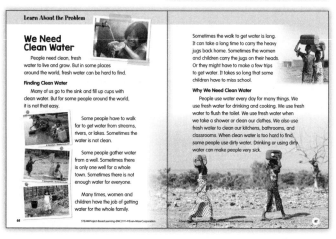

Art Connection

Prepare for the activity by asking students a few weeks in advance to bring in materials for the projects. You may wish to use the STEAM Materials Needed form on page 9 of this book. You will also need several adults to assist students. Give each student a copy of the Art Connection activity, "Music for the Rain," on pages 48–50 and read aloud the text and directions to them. Discuss each step in both projects and provide support as needed.

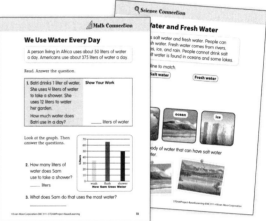

Math and Science Connections

Give each student a copy of the Math and Science Connection activities, "We Use Water Every Day" and "Salt Water and Fresh Water," on pages 51 and 52. Read aloud the directions, text, and items to them. Discuss the tasks and confirm understanding. Then have students complete the activities in small groups.

Career Spotlight

Give each student a copy of the Career Spotlight activity, "Helping Others Get Clean Water," on page 53. Have students discuss what they think the pictures may show. Then read aloud the text to students and have them complete the activity as a group.

STEAM Task

Prepare for the Steam Task by asking students a few weeks in advance to bring in materials for the project. You may wish to use the STEAM Materials Needed form on page 9 of this book. Give each student a copy of the STEAM Task on pages 54–57. Read aloud the Problem & Task page and confirm understanding. You may wish to have students work in small groups to do this task. Then guide students through the other stages of the design process and provide support as needed. After students finish, have them present their rainwater catchers to each other and explain how they made them.

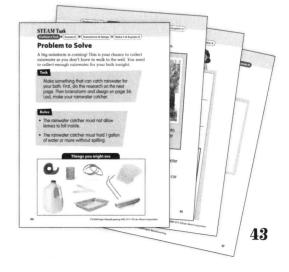

Read the story. Think about the problems in the story.

The Walk to the Well

Fatima lives in a small village in Africa. Her village does not have fresh water. Fatima has to travel a long way to get water from a well.

One morning before school, Fatima walked to the well to get water. Her family needed water to drink and to take a shower. It took Fatima many hours to get to the well. She filled her two big jugs with water and walked back home. Fatima held on tight to the jugs. But they were too heavy. She dropped them, and all the water spilled out.

Fatima walked back to the well and filled up her jugs. By the time she got back home with the water, school was over. Fatima started to cry. She loved going to school.

"Don't cry," said her friend Kenny. "I have an idea. Let's put buckets outside. It is supposed to rain tonight. They will catch the rain when it falls."

Kenny helped Fatima make a rainwater catcher. Fatima did not have to miss school the next day.

Problems Getting Water

Answer the items about the story you read.

1. Draw a picture of one problem you read in the story. Then finish the sentence about it.

One problem in the story is _____

_____.

2. How was the problem fixed?

This problem was fixed when _____

_____.

3. Can you think of another way to fix this problem?

I could fix this problem by _____

_____.

We Need Clean Water

People need clean, fresh water to live and grow. But in some places around the world, fresh water can be hard to find.

Finding Clean Water

Many of us go to the sink and fill up cups with clean water. But for some people around the world, it is not that easy.

© Martchan / Shutterstock.com

Some people have to walk far to get water from streams, rivers, or lakes. Sometimes the water is not clean.

© jennygiraffe / Shutterstock.com

Some people gather water from a well. Sometimes there is only one well for a whole town. Sometimes there is not enough water for everyone.

Many times, women and children have the job of getting water for the whole family.

Sometimes the walk to get water is long. It can take a long time to carry the heavy jugs back home. Sometimes the women and children carry the jugs on their heads. Or they might have to make a few trips to get water. It takes so long that some children have to miss school.

Why We Need Clean Water

People use water every day for many things. We use fresh water for drinking and cooking. We use fresh water to flush the toilet. We use fresh water when we take a shower or clean our clothes. We also use fresh water to clean our kitchens, bathrooms, and classrooms. When clean water is too hard to find, some people use dirty water. Drinking or using dirty water can make people very sick.

Music for the Rain

Some places need more rain so that the plants and animals have enough water. Some people use rainwater to take a bath. Some old stories tell about people who would dance and sing to celebrate rain.

You can make a musical instrument to celebrate rain like the people in the old stories. Make one or both of the instruments on the next pages. You can dance to the music you play on your new instruments!

What You Need

- See the directions for each instrument on the next pages.

What You Do

- Follow the directions on pages 49 and 50 to make your instruments.

Native American Rainstick

What You Need

- paper tube roll
- tape
- aluminum foil
- 2 muffin cups or 2 small pieces of paper
- dry beans, rice, or popcorn kernels
- markers, paint, stickers, or colored paper (optional)

What You Do

1. First, decorate the outside of your paper tube roll with markers, stickers, or fun shapes.

2. Next, tape a muffin cup or small piece of paper over one end of the tube roll.

3. Then, crumple a long piece of aluminum foil like a snake. Put the aluminum foil inside the tube.

4. Pour dry beans, rice, or popcorn kernels into the tube.

5. Last, tape the other muffin cup to the other end of the tube roll. Tip your rainstick back and forth to hear the sound of rain!

African Drum

- 2 paper cups
- scissors
- 1 plastic bag
- rubber band
- masking tape

- optional: string, markers, paint, stickers, or colored paper

What You Do

1. First, have an adult cut the bottoms out of both cups. Then tape the two bottoms together.

2. Next, cut a circle out of the plastic bag and stretch it over the top of one end of the cups. Use a rubber band to hold it in place. Cover it with masking tape for a strong hold.

3. Last, decorate the outside of your drum.

We Use Water Every Day

A person living in Africa uses about 50 liters of water a day. Americans use about 375 liters of water a day.

Read. Answer the question.

1. Batri drinks 1 liter of water. She uses 4 liters of water to take a shower. She uses 12 liters to water her garden.

How much water does Batri use in a day?

Show Your Work

_____ liters of water

Look at the graph. Then answer the questions.

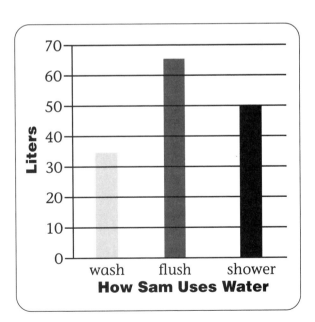

2. How many liters of water does Sam use to take a shower?

_____ liters

3. What does Sam do that uses the most water?

_____

Salt Water and Fresh Water

Earth has salt water and fresh water. People can drink fresh water. Fresh water comes from rivers, most lakes, ice, and rain. People cannot drink salt water. Salt water is found in oceans and some lakes.

1. Draw a line to match.

Salt water   Fresh water

 river

 ocean

 ice

2. Circle the body of water that can have salt water or fresh water.

Helping Others Get Clean Water

People all around the world work in jobs that make water clean or bring clean water to people who do not have it.

Read. Look at the picture.
Then draw a line to match.

These people dug a ditch for the water to run through.

These people build water wells.

These people learn how to keep the water in the wells clean.

Problem to Solve

A big rainstorm is coming! This is your chance to collect rainwater so you don't have to walk to the well. You need to collect enough rainwater for your bath tonight.

Task

Make something that can catch rainwater for your bath. First, do the research on the next page. Then brainstorm and design on page 56. Last, make your rainwater catcher.

Rules

- The rainwater catcher must not allow leaves to fall inside.

- The rainwater catcher must hold 1 gallon of water or more without spilling.

Things you might use

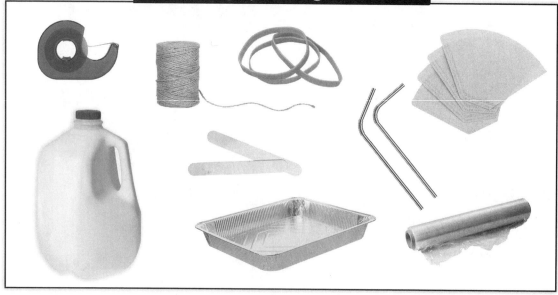

Keep Your Garden Safe

Read. Look at the pictures. Then answer the items.

roof

open pipe
shaped
like a taco

closed pipe

big bucket
to catch
rainwater

When rain falls on the roof of this house, it falls into the open pipe. Then a closed pipe leads the water down into a bucket.

1. Mark all the things you think this one bucket of water can be used for.

☐ bath ☐ brush teeth ☐ drink ☐ wash car

2. Can leaves and other items fall into the bucket?

○ yes ○ no

Rain Catcher Brainstorm

Answer these questions to help you brainstorm ideas to make a rain catcher.

1. Do you need a big or small bucket to catch the water?

   _____

2. What do you have that will let water through but keep leaves out?

   _____

Now draw a picture of what you will make to catch rainwater. Think about what you will use.

STEAM Project-Based Learning • EMC 3111 • © Evan-Moor Corporation

Make Your Rain Catcher

Make the rain catcher that you drew.

Then take a picture of it and glue it below.
Or draw a picture of your finished work in the box.

Mark the sentence that tells about what you made.

☐ The rain catcher I made can catch 1 gallon of water.

☐ The rain catcher I made cannot catch 1 gallon of water.

Finish the sentence.

I can _____ next
time to make my rain catcher better.

Recess

About the Topic

Many students look forward to recess. Playing with their friends, being outside, and playing games and sports is an important part of the day. However, not all students enjoy recess. Sometimes this is because they don't have friends, or they don't know how to play or are not good at playing the organized activities such as soccer or four square. As you introduce this topic to students, ask them to share their experiences and encourage them to tell how they feel about this problem.

Real-World Connection

Give each student a copy of the story "Fun on the Playground" on page 60. Read it aloud as they follow along silently. After you finish, you may wish to have them read the story independently or in small groups. Guide students in a discussion about the story and encourage them to share their thoughts and opinions.

What Is the Problem?

Give each student a copy of the activity on page 61, "Problems on the Playground." Read the directions and items aloud. Then have students complete the activity independently. After they finish, ask student volunteers to share their solutions about how to help with the problem.

Learn About the Problem

Give each student a copy of the nonfiction text, "Playtime at School," on pages 62 and 63. Read it aloud as they follow along silently. After you finish, you may wish to have them read the text independently or in small groups. Guide students in a discussion about the text and the pictures and encourage them to share their thoughts, feelings, and opinions.

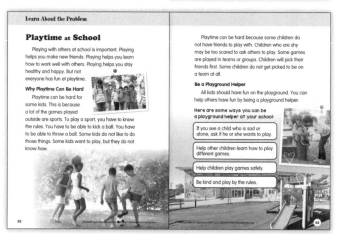

Art Connection

Give each student a copy of the Art Connection activity, "Dance Moves," on pages 64–66 and read aloud the text and directions to them. Model how to fold and glue the dance box cutout as students follow along. Then have students follow the directions to use their dance boxes. After they finish, you may wish to have students play with them in small groups.

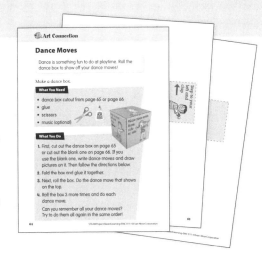

Math and Science Connections

Give each student a copy of the Math and Science Connection activities, "Kids on the Playground" and "Exercise on the Playground," on pages 67 and 68. Read aloud the text and items to them. Discuss the tasks and confirm understanding. Then have students complete the activities independently or in small groups.

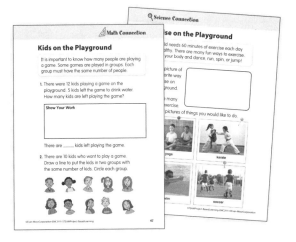

Career Spotlight

Give each student a copy of the Career Spotlight activity, "Dancers," on page 69. Explain what a career is and ask students to name different careers. Then have students look at each picture as you read each item aloud and have them complete the activity as a group.

STEAM Task

Give each student a copy of the STEAM Task on pages 70–73. Read aloud the Problem & Task page and confirm understanding. Provide support and materials as students complete the Research, Brainstorm & Design, and Make It & Explain It tasks. After they finish, you may wish to have students tell each other about the games they made.

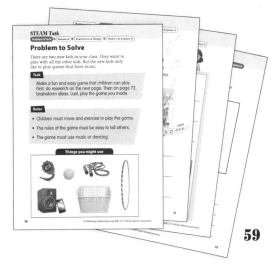

Read the story. Think about the problems in the story.

Fun on the Playground

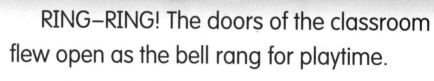

RING–RING! The doors of the classroom flew open as the bell rang for playtime.

Ruby walked out of the classroom slowly. She wanted to run. She wanted to play. But she did not have friends to play with.

Ruby saw kids play basketball. It looked fun. But Ruby did not know how to play. Ruby saw kids play soccer. She wanted to play. But Ruby did not think she was good at sports. This made Ruby sad. She had nothing to do.

Then Ruby heard music. She saw kids dancing. "I know how to dance!" said Ruby.

Ruby danced. Ruby smiled. Ruby made new friends. Ruby had a lot of fun on the playground.

STEAM Project-Based Learning • EMC 3111 • © Evan-Moor Corporation

Problems on the Playground

Answer the items about the story you read.

1. Draw a picture of one problem you read in the story. Then write a sentence about it.

One problem in the story is _____

_____.

2. Who does this problem hurt?

This problem hurts _____

_____.

3. How can you help with this problem?

I can help by _____

_____.

Playtime at School

Playing with others at school is important. Playing helps you make new friends. Playing helps you learn how to work well with others. Playing helps you stay healthy and happy. But not everyone has fun at playtime.

Why Playtime Can Be Hard

Playtime can be hard for some kids. This is because a lot of the games played outside are sports. To play a sport, you have to know the rules. You have to be able to kick a ball. You have to be able to throw a ball. Some kids do not like to do those things. Some kids want to play, but they do not know how.

Playtime can be hard because some children do not have friends to play with. Children who are shy may be too scared to ask others to play. Some games are played in teams or groups. Children will pick their friends first. Some children do not get picked to be on a team at all.

Be a Playground Helper

All kids should have fun on the playground. You can help others have fun by being a playground helper.

Here are some ways you can be a playground helper at your school:

> If you see a child who is sad or alone, ask if he or she wants to play.

> Help other children learn how to play different games.

> Help children play games safely.

> Be kind and play by the rules.

Dance Moves

Dance is something fun to do at playtime. Roll the dance box to show off your dance moves!

Make a dance box.

What You Need

- dance box cutout from page 65 or page 66
- glue
- scissors
- music (optional)

What You Do

1. First, cut out the dance box on page 65 or cut out the blank one on page 66. If you use the blank one, write dance moves and draw pictures on it. Then follow the directions below.

2. Fold the box and glue it together.

3. Next, roll the box. Do the dance move that shows on the top.

4. Roll the box 3 more times and do each dance move.

   Can you remember all your dance moves? Try to do them all again in the same order!

Spin around 2 times

Wiggle your whole body

Step to your left and clap

Step to your right and clap

Wave your arms from side to side

Hop 3 times

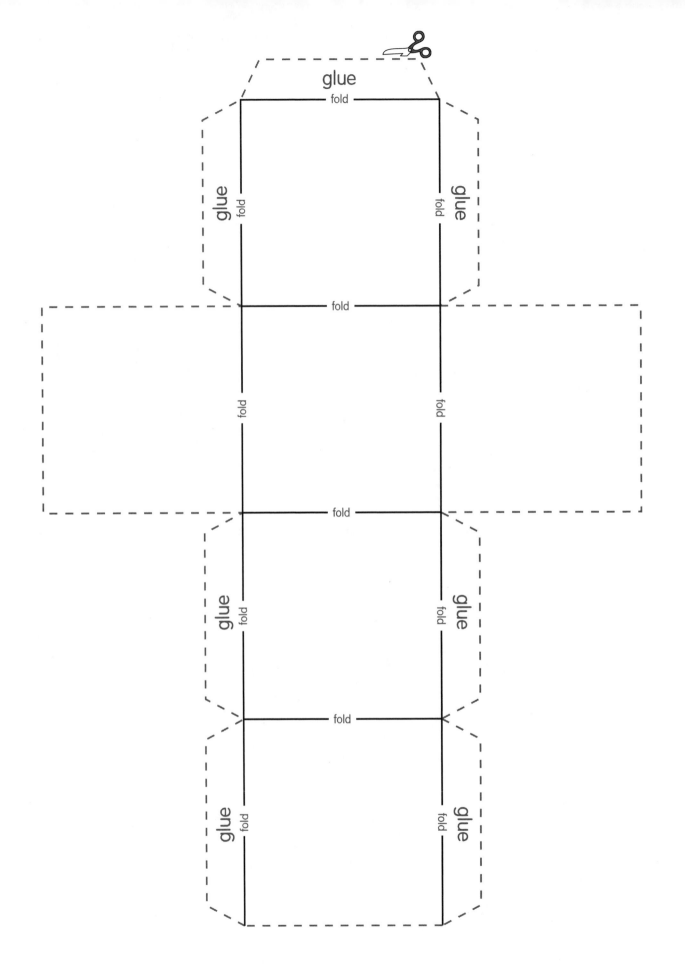

Kids on the Playground

It is important to know how many people are playing a game. Some games are played in groups. Each group must have the same number of people.

1. There were 12 kids playing a game on the playground. 5 kids left the game to drink water. How many kids are left playing the game?

Show Your Work

There are _____ kids left playing the game.

2. There are 10 kids who want to play a game. Draw a line to put the kids in two groups with the same number of kids. Circle each group.

Exercise on the Playground

Every child needs 60 minutes of exercise each day to be healthy. There are many fun ways to exercise. So move your body and dance, run, spin, or jump!

1. Draw a picture of your favorite way to exercise on the playground.

2. There are many ways to exercise. Circle the pictures of things you would like to do.

yoga

karate

swim

soccer

Dancers

A dancer is a person who tells a story with his or her body. A dancer moves his or her body parts to music to tell you how he or she feels.

Draw a line to match.

●

These dancers use moves that you see on the street or on TV.

●

These dancers use a special shoe to make sounds.

●

These dancers use light and soft moves. Some dance on the tips of their toes.

Problem to Solve

There are two new kids in your class. They want to play with all the other kids. But the new kids only like to play games that have music.

Task

Make a fun and easy game that children can play. First, do research on the next page. Then on page 72, brainstorm ideas. Last, play the game you made.

Rules

- Children must move and exercise to play the game.

- The rules of the game must be easy to tell others.

- The game must use music or dancing.

Things you might use

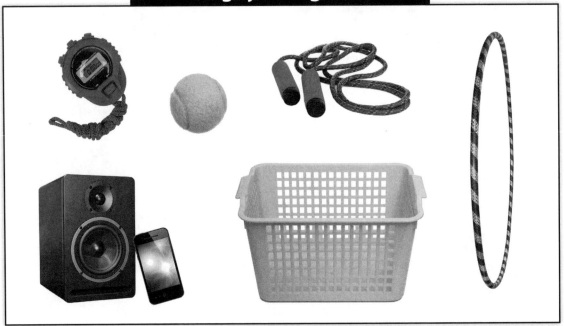

STEAM Project-Based Learning • EMC 3111 • © Evan-Moor Corporation

Games for All

Read about a game. Look at the picture.
Then answer the questions.

This game is called Music Tag. Any number of people can play. You have to tag as many people as you can while a song plays. If someone tags you, you must stop and do 10 jumping jacks before you can play again. The person who tags the most people by the end of the song wins!

1. How many people can play this game?

_____

2. Are the rules of the game easy to learn?

_____

3. Does this game make people exercise?

_____

Game Brainstorm

Answer these questions to help you
brainstorm ideas for your game.

1. What things do you need to play your
   game?

   _____

2. How many people can play this game?

   _____

3. How do you win this game?

   _____

Now draw a picture of what your game will look like.
Think about what you will use.

STEAM Project-Based Learning • EMC 3111 • © Evan-Moor Corporation

Game Time

Play the game you made up. Then take a picture of you playing the game and glue the picture below.

Or draw a picture of you playing the game.

Finish the sentences to tell more about your game.

My game is called _____.

This game is fun because _____

_____

_____

_____.

Gardens and Animal Safety

About the Topic

People grow flowers, fruits, vegetables, and other plants in their gardens. Some people grow gardens for pleasure, and other people grow gardens in order to have food to eat. No matter the reason for growing a garden, people have to protect their plants from hungry animals that are looking for something to eat. It is equally important to make sure the animals are not harmed in the process. Ask students to share what they know about gardens and if they have seen animals in a garden.

Real-World Connection

Give each student a copy of the story "Missing Strawberries" on page 76. Read it aloud as they follow along silently. After you finish, you may wish to have them read the story independently or in small groups. Guide students in a discussion about the story and encourage them to share their thoughts and opinions.

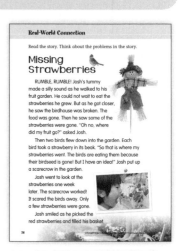

What Is the Problem?

Give each student a copy of the activity on page 77, "Problems in the Garden." Read the directions and items aloud. Then have students complete the activity independently. After they finish, ask student volunteers to share their solutions about how to help with the problem.

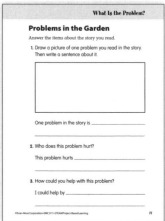

Learn About the Problem

Give each student a copy of the nonfiction text, "Animals in the Garden," on pages 78 and 79. Read it aloud as they follow along silently. After you finish, you may wish to have them read the text independently or in small groups. Guide students in a discussion about the text and the pictures and encourage them to share their thoughts and opinions.

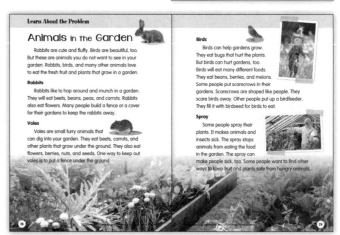

Art Connection

Give each student a copy of the Art Connection activity, "Mini Scarecrow," on pages 80–82 and read aloud the text and directions to them. Discuss each step in the project and provide support as needed.

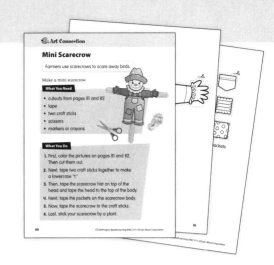

Science and Technology Connections

Give each student a copy of the Science and Technology Connection activities, "What Plants Need" and "Gardening Tools," on pages 83 and 84. Read aloud the text and items to them. Discuss the tasks and confirm understanding. Then have students complete the activities independently or in small groups.

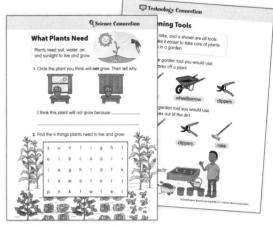

Career Spotlight

Give each student a copy of the Career Spotlight activity, "Gardeners," on page 85. Explain what a career is and ask students to name different careers. Then read aloud the text to students. Guide students in a discussion about what gardeners do and how they can help keep animals that visit gardens safe. Lastly, have students complete the item at the bottom of the page.

STEAM Task

Prepare for the STEAM Task by asking students a few weeks in advance to bring in materials for the project. You may wish to use the STEAM Materials Needed form on page 9 of this book. Give each student a copy of the STEAM Task on pages 86–89. Read aloud the Problem & Task page and confirm understanding. Guide students to do the Research, Brainstorm & Design, and Make It & Explain It tasks. You may wish to have students present their completed projects to each other.

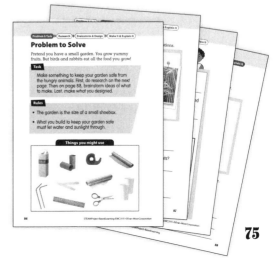

Read the story. Think about the problems in the story.

Missing Strawberries

RUMBLE, RUMBLE! Josh's tummy made a silly sound as he walked to his fruit garden. He could not wait to eat the strawberries he grew. But as he got closer, he saw the birdhouse was broken. The food was gone. Then he saw some of the strawberries were gone. "Oh no, where did my fruit go?" asked Josh.

Then two birds flew down into the garden. Each bird took a strawberry in its beak. "So that is where my strawberries went. The birds are eating them because their birdseed is gone! But I have an idea!" Josh put up a scarecrow in the garden.

Josh went to look at the strawberries one week later. The scarecrow worked! It scared the birds away. Only a few strawberries were gone.

Josh smiled as he picked the red strawberries and filled his basket.

Problems in the Garden

Answer the items about the story you read.

1. Draw a picture of one problem you read in the story. Then write a sentence about it.

```
┌─────────────────────────────────────────────┐
│                                             │
│                                             │
│                                             │
│                                             │
│                                             │
│                                             │
│                                             │
└─────────────────────────────────────────────┘
```

One problem in the story is _____

_____.

2. Who does this problem hurt?

This problem hurts _____

_____.

3. How could you help with this problem?

I could help by _____

_____.

Animals in the Garden

Rabbits are cute and fluffy. Birds are beautiful, too. But these are animals you do not want to see in your garden. Rabbits, birds, and many other animals love to eat the fresh fruit and plants that grow in a garden.

Rabbits

Rabbits like to hop around and munch in a garden. They will eat beets, beans, peas, and carrots. Rabbits also eat flowers. Many people build a fence or a cover for their gardens to keep the rabbits away.

Voles

Voles are small furry animals that can dig into your garden. They eat beets, carrots, and other plants that grow under the ground. They also eat flowers, berries, nuts, and seeds. One way to keep out voles is to put a fence under the ground.

Birds

Birds can help gardens grow. They eat bugs that hurt the plants. But birds can hurt gardens, too. Birds will eat many different foods. They eat beans, berries, and melons. Some people put scarecrows in their gardens. Scarecrows are shaped like people. They scare birds away. Other people put up a bird feeder. They fill it with birdseed for birds to eat.

Spray

Some people spray their plants. It makes animals and insects sick. The spray stops animals from eating the food in the garden. The spray can make people sick, too. Some people want to find other ways to keep fruit and plants safe from hungry animals.

Mini Scarecrow

Farmers use scarecrows to scare away birds.

Make a mini scarecrow.

What You Need

- cutouts from pages 81 and 82
- tape
- two craft sticks
- scissors
- markers or crayons

What You Do

1. First, color the pictures on pages 81 and 82. Then cut them out.

2. Next, tape two craft sticks together to make a lowercase "t."

3. Then, tape the scarecrow hat on top of the head and tape the head to the top of the body.

4. Next, tape the pockets on the scarecrow body.

5. Now, tape the scarecrow to the craft sticks.

6. Last, stick your scarecrow by a plant.

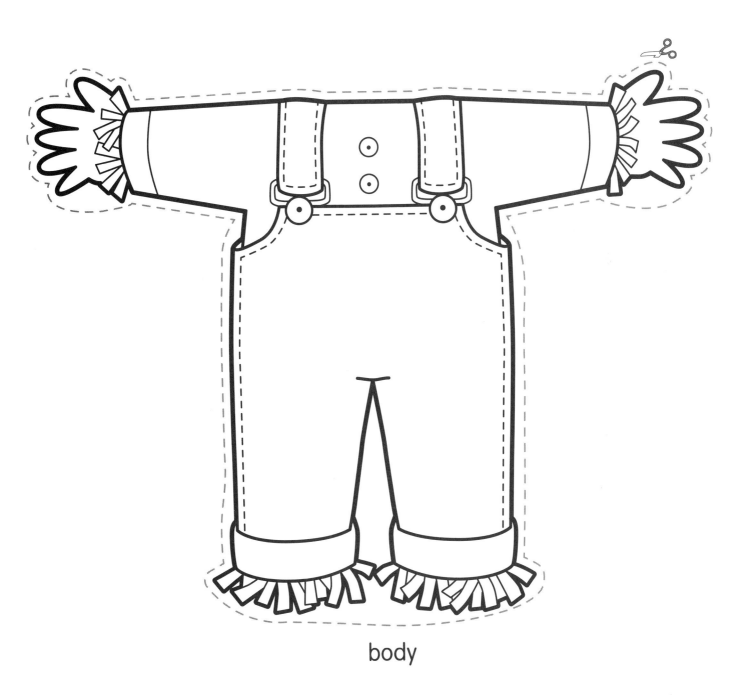

body

hat

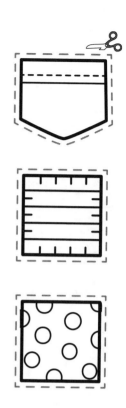

pockets

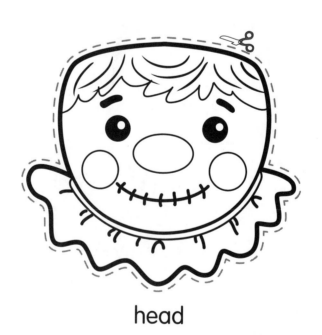

head

What Plants Need

Plants need soil, water, air, and sunlight to live and grow.

1. Circle the plant you think will **not** grow. Then tell why.

I think this plant will not grow because _____

_____ .

2. Find the 4 things plants need to live and grow.

s	u	n	l	i	g	h	t
o	l	b	c	a	a	i	r
i	e	g	h	t	d	f	k
l	e	w	a	t	e	r	j
p	n	k	t	w	t	e	r

Gardening Tools

A hoe, a rake, and a shovel are all tools. Tools make it easier to take care of plants and work in a garden.

1. Circle the garden tool you would use to cut leaves off a plant.

rake   wheelbarrow   clippers

2. Circle the garden tool you would use to get leaves out of the dirt.

shovel   clippers   rake

Gardeners

Some people know a lot about plants and how they grow. They plan gardens and work in them. They also think of how to use plants to help sick people feel better.

Carrot flies are bugs that hurt carrots by eating carrot roots. The flies also eat dill. They like the smell of carrots, but do not like the smell of garlic and onions. They stay away from smells they do not like.

Help the gardener plan which food to plant next to the carrots. Circle the food that will help the carrots grow. Then tell why.

celery

onion

_____

_____

Problem to Solve

Pretend you have a small garden. You grow yummy fruits. But birds and rabbits eat all the food you grow!

Task

Make something to keep your garden safe from the hungry animals. First, do research on the next page. Then on page 88, brainstorm ideas of what to make. Last, make what you designed.

Rules

- The garden is the size of a small shoebox.

- What you build to keep your garden safe must let water and sunlight through.

Things you might use

Keep Your Garden Safe

Read. Look at the pictures. Then answer the questions.

This wood fence was
made to keep the plants safe.

1. How does this fence keep the plants safe from
animals?

_____

2. Are there any animals that could still eat the plants?

_____

3. Can the plants get everything they need to live
and grow?

_____

Safe Garden Brainstorm

Answer these questions to help you brainstorm ideas to keep your garden safe.

1. What do plants need to grow?

_____

2. Which animals do you think will try to eat the food from your garden?

_____

Now draw a picture of what you will make to keep your garden safe. Think about what you will use.

STEAM Project-Based Learning • EMC 3111 • © Evan-Moor Corporation

Problem & Task → Research → Brainstorm & Design → **Make It & Explain It**

Make Your Garden Safe

Make what you drew to keep the garden safe.

Then take a picture of it and glue the picture below. Or draw a picture of your finished work in the box.

Finish the sentences to tell more about what you made.

I made this to keep ____________ and

____________ out of my garden.

This is how it works:

____

____

____.

Moving to a New Place

About the Topic

When people move to a new place that has a different culture and language, it can be difficult for them to feel welcome or feel that they fit it. Sometimes a community welcomes new members and sometimes they fall short of having a welcoming attitude to people who look, speak, dress, and eat differently than they do. This situation can be especially difficult for children who are attending a new school. As you introduce this topic to students, invite them to share their experiences.

Real-World Connection

Give each student a copy of the story "The New Kid" on page 92. Read it aloud as they follow along silently. After you finish, you may wish to have them read the story independently or in small groups. Guide students in a discussion about the story and encourage them to share their thoughts and feelings.

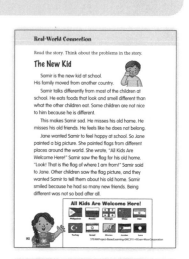

What Is the Problem?

Give each student a copy of the activity on page 93, "The New Kid's Problems." Read the directions and items aloud. Then have students complete the activity independently. After they finish, ask student volunteers to share their solutions about how to help with the problem.

Learn About the Problem

Give each student a copy of the nonfiction text, "Moving to a New Place," on pages 94 and 95. Read it aloud as they follow along silently. After you finish, you may wish to have them read the text independently or in small groups. Guide students in a discussion about the text and the pictures and encourage them to share their thoughts and opinions.

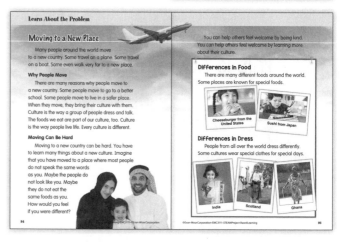

Art Connection

Give each student a copy of the Art Connection activity, "Culture Drawings," on pages 96–98 and read aloud the text and directions to them. You may wish to send this activity for students to complete with their family. After they finish, have them bring it to school. Then plan a time for students to present what they created, or make a bulletin board display for students' completed activities.

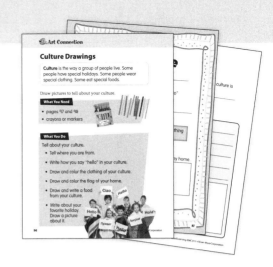

Technology and Science Connections

Give each student a copy of the Technology and Science Connection activities, "Travel Around the World" and "Pickled Food Science," on pages 99 and 100. Read aloud the directions, text, and items to them. Discuss the tasks and confirm understanding. Then have students complete the activities independently or in small groups.

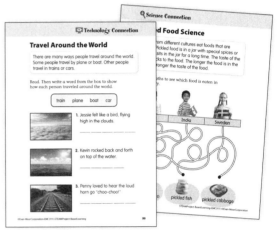

Career Spotlight

Give each student a copy of the Career Spotlight activity, "Artists," on page 101. Explain what a career is and ask students to name different careers. Then read aloud the text to students. Guide students in a discussion about how different artists create different forms of art. Then have them complete the drawing task.

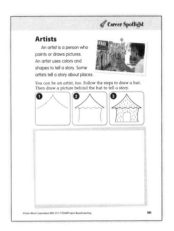

STEAM Task

Give each student a copy of the STEAM Task on pages 102–105. Read aloud the Problem & Task page and confirm understanding. You may wish to have students work in small groups to do the Research task. Then guide students to do the Brainstorm & Design and Make It & Explain It tasks independently. You may wish to have students present their completed drawings to each other.

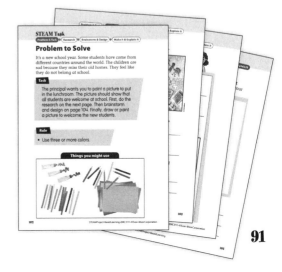

Read the story. Think about the problems in the story.

The New Kid

Samir is the new kid at school. His family moved from another country.

Samir talks differently from most of the children at school. He eats foods that look and smell different than what the other children eat. Some children are not nice to him because he is different.

This makes Samir sad. He misses his old home. He misses his old friends. He feels like he does not belong.

Jane wanted Samir to feel happy at school. So Jane painted a big picture. She painted flags from different places around the world. She wrote, "All Kids Are Welcome Here!" Samir saw the flag for his old home. "Look! That is the flag of where I am from!" Samir said to Jane. Other children saw the flag picture, and they wanted Samir to tell them about his old home. Samir smiled because he had so many new friends. Being different was not so bad after all.

All Kids Are Welcome Here!

Philippines Russia Georgia China Iran

Turkey Israel Bhutan Jordan Laos

STEAM Project-Based Learning • EMC 3111 • © Evan-Moor Corporation

The New Kid's Problems

Answer the items about the story you read.

1. Draw a picture of one problem you read in the story. Then finish the sentence about it.

One problem in the story is _____

_____.

2. How was the problem fixed?

This problem was fixed when _____

_____.

3. What is another way you could help with this problem?

I could help by _____

_____.

Moving to a New Place

Many people around the world move to a new country. Some travel on a plane. Some travel on a boat. Some even walk very far to a new place.

Why People Move

There are many reasons why people move to a new country. Some people move to go to a better school. Some people move to live in a safer place. When they move, they bring their culture with them. Culture is the way a group of people dress and talk. The foods we eat are part of our culture, too. Culture is the way people live life. Every culture is different.

Moving Can Be Hard

Moving to a new country can be hard. You have to learn many things about a new culture. Imagine that you have moved to a place where most people do not speak the same words as you. Maybe the people do not look like you. Maybe they do not eat the same foods as you. How would you feel if you were different?

You can help others feel welcome by being kind. You can help others feel welcome by learning more about their culture.

Differences in Food

There are many different foods around the world. Some places are known for special foods.

Cheeseburger from the United States

Sushi from Japan

Differences in Dress

People from all over the world dress differently. Some cultures wear special clothes for special days.

India

Scotland

Ghana

Culture Drawings

Culture is the way a group of people live. Some people have special holidays. Some people wear special clothing. Some eat special foods.

Draw pictures to tell about your culture.

What You Need

- pages 97 and 98
- crayons or markers

What You Do

Tell about your culture.

- Tell where you are from.

- Write how you say "hello" in your culture.

- Draw and color the clothing of your culture.

- Draw and color the flag of your home.

- Draw and write a food from your culture.

- Write about your favorite holiday. Draw a picture about it.

My Culture

I am from _____.

How to say "hello"
in my culture:

_____

This is the clothing
of my culture.

This is the flag of my home.

My Culture

One food of my culture is

_____.

The holiday I like the most is called _____.

I like this holiday because _____

_____

_____

_____.

Travel Around the World

There are many ways people travel around the world. Some people travel by plane or boat. Other people travel in trains or cars.

Read. Then write a word from the box to show how each person traveled around the world.

train   plane   boat   car

1. Jessie felt like a bird, flying high in the clouds.

____ ____ ____ ____

2. Kevin rocked back and forth on top of the water.

____ ____ ____ ____

3. Penny loved to hear the loud horn go "choo-choo!"

____ ____ ____ ____

Pickled Food Science

People from different cultures eat foods that are pickled. Pickled food is in a jar with special spices or sauce. It sits in the jar for a long time. The taste of the sauce sticks to the food. The longer the food is in the jar, the stronger the taste of the food.

Trace the paths to see which food is eaten in each country.

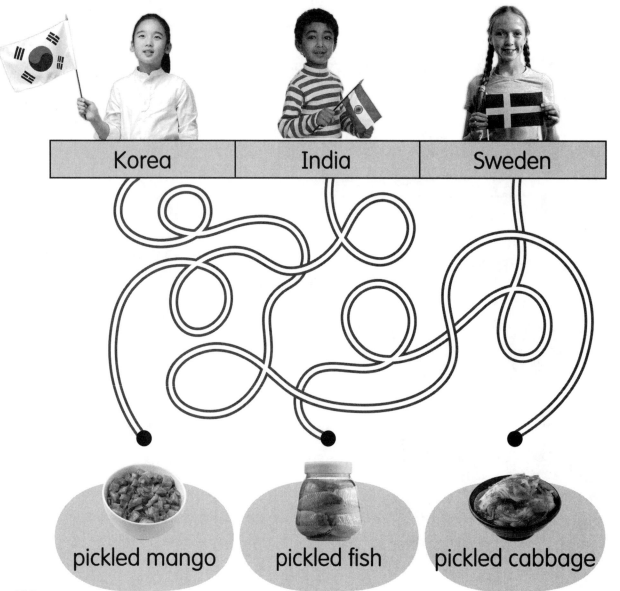

| Korea | India | Sweden |

pickled mango   pickled fish   pickled cabbage

Artists

An artist is a person who paints or draws pictures. An artist uses colors and shapes to tell a story. Some artists tell a story about places.

You can be an artist, too. Follow the steps to draw a hut. Then draw a picture behind the hut to tell a story.

 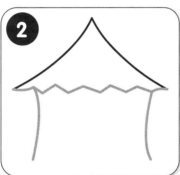 

Problem to Solve

It's a new school year. Some students have come from different countries around the world. The children are sad because they miss their old homes. They feel like they do not belong at school.

Task

The principal wants you to paint a picture to put in the lunchroom. The picture should show that all students are welcome at school. First, do the research on the next page. Then brainstorm and design on page 104. Finally, draw or paint a picture to welcome the new students.

Rule

• Use three or more colors.

Things you might use

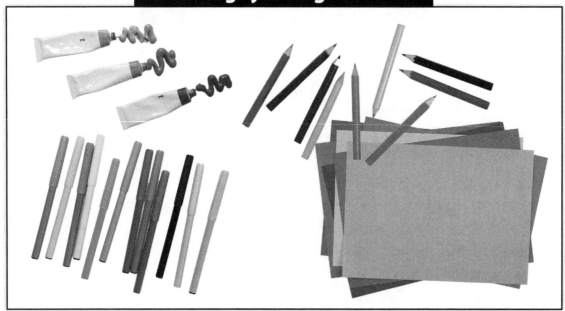

School Wall Art

Look at the painting. Then answer the questions.

© Rxlaker

1. How do you feel when you look at the painting?

_____

2. Why do you think the artist painted this picture?

_____

3. Would this painting make a child feel welcome at a new school? Tell why or why not.

_____

_____

School Art Brainstorm

Answer these questions to help you brainstorm ideas for your picture.

1. Why are you drawing this art?

   _____

2. What colors make you feel happy?

   _____

3. Draw a picture of things you can do to make others feel happy.

Welcome–to–School Art

Paint or draw your school wall art on a small sheet of paper. Then glue it below. Or draw a picture of your art below.

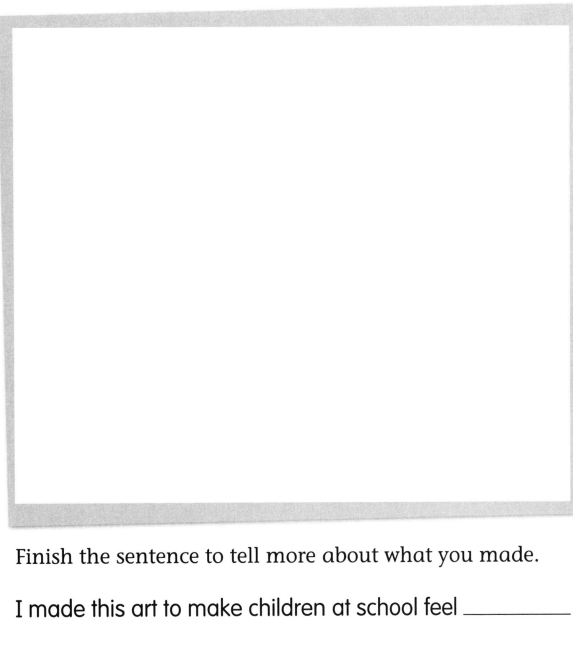

Finish the sentence to tell more about what you made.

I made this art to make children at school feel _____

_____

_____.

Walk to School

About the Topic

In many parts of the world, children have to walk long distances to get to school. Sometimes the route to school has difficult and dangerous terrain, but children still go because they are determined to get an education. As you introduce this topic to students, consider their own experiences with transportation to school. They may not have imagined that some students have to walk really long distances to get to school. Invite students to ask any questions they have about this problem.

Real-World Connection

Give each student a copy of the story "The Long Walk to School" on page 108. Read it aloud as they follow along silently. After you finish, you may wish to have them read the story independently or in small groups. Guide students in a discussion about the story and encourage them to share their thoughts and opinions.

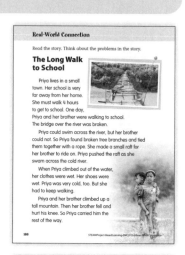

What Is the Problem?

Give each student a copy of the activity on page 109, "Problems on the Long Walk." Read the directions and items aloud. Then have students complete the activity independently. After they finish, ask student volunteers to share their solutions about how to help with the problem.

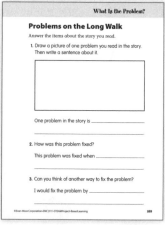

Learn About the Problem

Give each student a copy of the nonfiction text, "Travel to Far-Away Schools," on pages 110 and 111. Read it aloud as they follow along silently. After you finish, you may wish to have them read the text independently or in small groups. Guide students in a discussion about the text and the pictures and encourage them to share their thoughts and opinions.

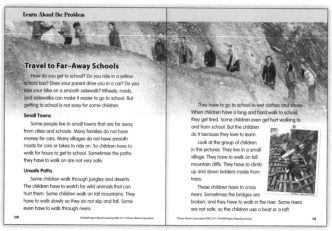

Art Connection

Prepare for the activity by asking students a few weeks in advance to bring in materials for the project. You may wish to use the STEAM Materials Needed form on page 9 of this book. Give each student a copy of pages 112–114 and read aloud the text and directions to them. Meet with students in small groups and discuss each step in the project. You may need a few adults to provide guidance and support as students complete each step. Encourage students to be creative and use their imaginations to make a guard statue.

Math and Engineering Connections

Give each student a copy of the Math and Engineering Connection activities, "Time for School" and "Getting to School," on pages 115 and 116. Read aloud the directions, text, and items to them. Discuss the tasks and confirm understanding. Then have students complete the activities independently or in small groups.

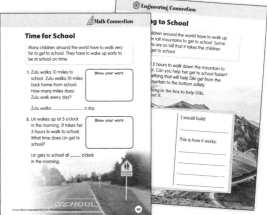

Career Spotlight

Give each student a copy of the Career Spotlight activity on page 117. Explain what a career is and ask students to name different careers. Then read aloud the text to students. Guide students in a discussion about what civil engineers do and the things they build. Lastly, have students complete the color-by-number activity.

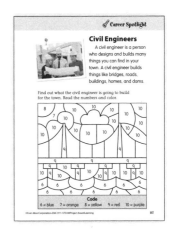

STEAM Task

Prepare for the STEAM Task by asking students a few weeks in advance to bring in materials for the project. You may wish to use the STEAM Materials Needed form on page 9 of this book. Give each student a copy of the STEAM Task on pages 118–121. Read aloud the Problem & Task page and confirm understanding. You may wish to have students work in small groups to do this task. Then guide students through the other stages of the design process and provide support as needed. After students finish, have them present their projects to each other and explain how they made them.

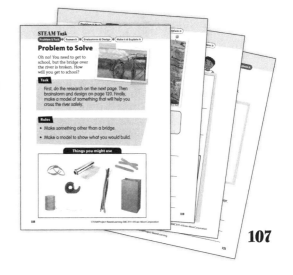

Read the story. Think about the problems in the story.

The Long Walk to School

Priya lives in a small town. Her school is very far away from her home. She must walk 4 hours to get to school. One day, Priya and her brother were walking to school. The bridge over the river was broken.

Priya could swim across the river, but her brother could not. So Priya found broken tree branches and tied them together with a rope. She made a small raft for her brother to ride on. Priya pushed the raft as she swam across the cold river.

When Priya climbed out of the water, her clothes were wet. Her shoes were wet. Priya was very cold, too. But she had to keep walking.

Priya and her brother climbed up a tall mountain. Then her brother fell and hurt his knee. So Priya carried him the rest of the way.

Problems on the Long Walk

Answer the items about the story you read.

1. Draw a picture of one problem you read in the story. Then write a sentence about it.

One problem in the story is _____

_____.

2. How was this problem fixed?

This problem was fixed when _____

_____.

3. Can you think of another way to fix the problem?

I would fix the problem by _____

_____.

Travel to Far–Away Schools

How do you get to school? Do you ride in a yellow school bus? Does your parent drive you in a car? Do you ride your bike on a smooth sidewalk? Wheels, roads, and sidewalks can make it easier to go to school. But getting to school is not easy for some children.

Small Towns

Some people live in small towns that are far away from cities and schools. Many families do not have money for cars. Many villages do not have smooth roads for cars or bikes to ride on. So children have to walk for hours to get to school. Sometimes the paths they have to walk on are not very safe.

Unsafe Paths

Some children walk through jungles and deserts. The children have to watch for wild animals that can hurt them. Some children walk on tall mountains. They have to walk slowly so they do not slip and fall. Some even have to walk through rivers.

They have to go to school in wet clothes and shoes.
When children have a long and hard walk to school,
they get tired. Some children even get hurt walking to
and from school. But the children
do it because they love to learn.

Look at the group of children
in the pictures. They live in a small
village. They have to walk on tall
mountain cliffs. They have to climb
up and down ladders made from
trees.

These children have to cross
rivers. Sometimes the bridges are

© Xinhua / Alamy Stock Photo

broken, and they have to walk in the river. Some rivers
are not safe, so the children use a boat or a raft.

Guard Statues

A **statue** (sta-choo) is art that is made out of metal, wood, stone, or something else. Statues can be in the shape of people or animals. Some people believe that statues can keep us safe. These people use guard statues. When you guard something, you keep it safe. People put guard statues in front of their homes and buildings.

Help children stay safe on their long walks to school. Make your own statue to guard the path for the children.

Step 1: Brainstorm

- Think about what animal or person can keep the path safe.

- Think about what animal or person would make children feel safe.

Look at the pictures below and on page 112.
Then answer the questions.

Step 2: Do Research

- What shape are the statues?

- Why do you think someone chose these people or animals to guard the buildings?

- Do the statues have faces?

- Are the faces smiling or frowning?

© Joymsk140 / Shutterstock.com

Step 3: Plan

Choose the things you want to use to make your statue. These are things you might use:

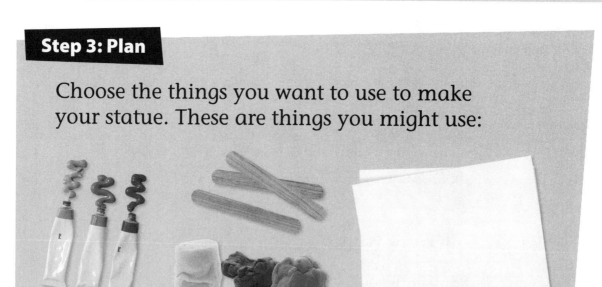

Draw a picture of the statue you would like to make. Think about the materials you chose.

Step 4: Make It and Share It

Make your statue. Then show it to a friend. Tell your friend why you made it.

STEAM Project-Based Learning • EMC 3111 • © Evan-Moor Corporation

Time for School

Many children around the world have to walk very far to get to school. They have to wake up early to be at school on time.

1. Zulu walks 10 miles to school. Zulu walks 10 miles back home from school. How many miles does Zulu walk every day?

Show your work

Zulu walks _____ a day.

2. Lin wakes up at 5 o'clock in the morning. It takes her 3 hours to walk to school. What time does Lin get to school?

Show your work

Lin gets to school at _____ o'clock in the morning.

Getting to School

Many children around the world have to walk up and down tall mountains to get to school. Some mountains are so tall that it takes the children hours to get to school.

It takes Diki 2 hours to walk down the mountain to get to school. Can you help her get to school faster? Design something that will help Diki get from the top of the mountain to the bottom safely.

Draw something in the box to help Diki. Then tell about it.

I would build

_____.

This is how it works:

_____

_____

_____

_____

STEAM Project Based Learning • EMC 3111 • © Evan-Moor Corporation

Civil Engineers

A civil engineer is a person who designs and builds many things you can find in your town. A civil engineer builds things like bridges, roads, buildings, homes, and dams.

Find out what the civil engineer is going to build for the town. Read the numbers and color.

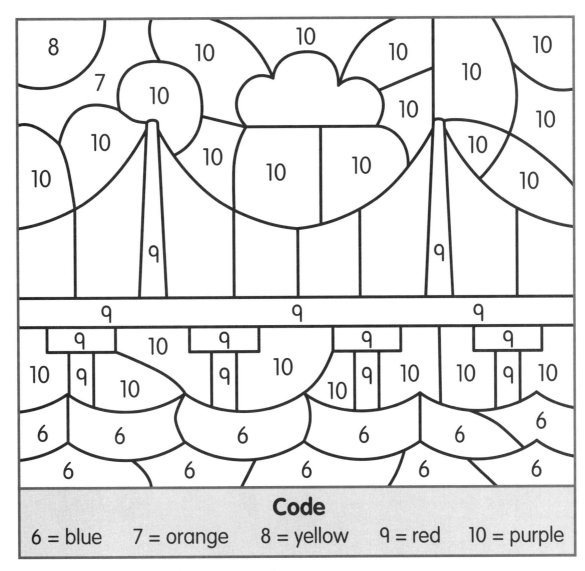

Code

6 = blue   7 = orange   8 = yellow   9 = red   10 = purple

Problem to Solve

Oh no! You need to get to school, but the bridge over the river is broken. How will you get to school?

Task

First, do the research on the next page. Then brainstorm and design on page 120. Finally, make a model of something that will help you cross the river safely.

Rules

- Make something other than a bridge.

- Make a model to show what you would build.

Things you might use

Walking on Ropes

Read. Look at the pictures.
Then answer the questions.

© geoff wiggins / Alamy Stock Photo / Alamy Stock Photo

© geoff wiggins / Alamy Stock Photo / Alamy Stock Photo

These people cross over a river by riding in a box.
A strong rope holds up the box. You must pull
on the rope to move the box to the other side.

1. What do you like about this way to travel?

_____

2. What do you not like about this way to travel?

_____

3. Would you ride in this box? Why or why not?

_____

_____

Crossing the River Brainstorm

Answer these items to help you brainstorm
different ways to cross a river.

1. What are some ways to cross a river
that you already know about?
Write one way to cross on the line.

_____

2. Think of a fun new way to cross a river.
Write it on the line.

_____

Now draw a picture of what you will make to
cross the river. Think about what you will use.

STEAM Project-Based Learning • EMC 3111 • © Evan-Moor Corporation

Getting to School

Make a model of what you drew to cross the river.

Then take a picture of it and glue the picture below.
Or draw a picture of what you made in the box.

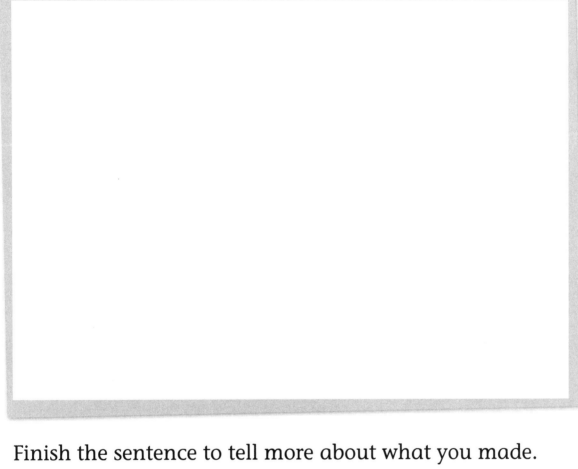

Finish the sentence to tell more about what you made.

I made a _____ to cross the river.

Write to tell how it works.

_____

_____

_____

Congratulations!

_____
Name

You went
FULL **STEAM** AHEAD
to solve problems!

 Science

 Technology

 Engineering

 Art

Math

Cut out the pieces. Put them together to find out what the picture shows.
Then glue them onto construction paper to make a poster.

NEERING

ART

GY ENGIN

Answer Key

Page 19

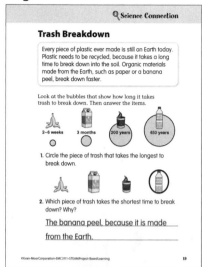

Trash Breakdown

Every piece of plastic ever made is still on Earth today. Plastic needs to be recycled, because it takes a long time to break down into the soil. Organic materials made from the Earth, such as paper or a banana peel, break down faster.

Look at the bubbles that show how long it takes trash to break down. Then answer the items.

2–6 weeks   3 months   200 years   450 years

1. Circle the piece of trash that takes the longest to break down.

2. Which piece of trash takes the shortest time to break down? Why?
   The banana peel, because it is made from the Earth.

Page 20

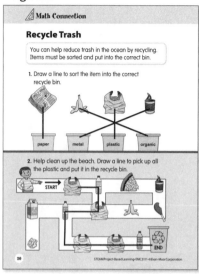

Recycle Trash

You can help reduce trash in the ocean by recycling. Items must be sorted and put into the correct bin.

1. Draw a line to sort the item into the correct recycle bin.

paper   metal   plastic   organic

2. Help clean up the beach. Draw a line to pick up all the plastic and put it in the recycle bin.

START   END

Page 35

Signs That Help

Signs are tools that help tell us things we need to know.

Look at the signs. Write what you think each sign wants you to know.

1. stop
2. bathroom
3. throw away your trash

Draw your own sign. Then tell what it means.

4. Answers will vary.

Page 36

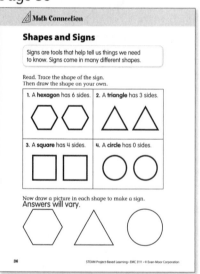

Shapes and Signs

Signs are tools that help us tell us things we need to know. Signs come in many different shapes.

Read. Trace the shape of the sign. Then draw the shape on your own.

1. A **hexagon** has 6 sides.
2. A **triangle** has 3 sides.
3. A **square** has 4 sides.
4. A **circle** has 0 sides.

Now draw a picture in each shape to make a sign.
Answers will vary.

Page 51

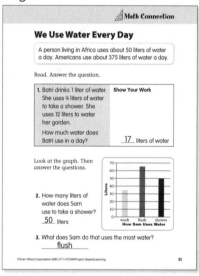

We Use Water Every Day

A person living in Africa uses about 50 liters of water a day. Americans use about 375 liters of water a day.

Read. Answer the question.

1. Batri drinks 1 liter of water. She uses 4 liters of water to take a shower. She uses 12 liters to water her garden.
   How much water does Batri use in a day?
   Show Your Work
   17 liters of water

Look at the graph. Then answer the questions.

2. How many liters of water does Sam use to take a shower?
   50 liters

3. What does Sam do that uses the most water?
   flush

How Sam Uses Water

Page 52

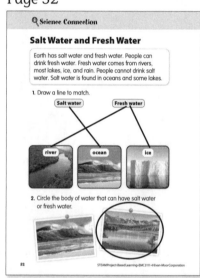

Salt Water and Fresh Water

Earth has salt water and fresh water. People can drink fresh water. Fresh water comes from rivers, most lakes, ice, and rain. People cannot drink salt water. Salt water is found in oceans and some lakes.

1. Draw a line to match.

Salt water   Fresh water

river   ocean   ice

2. Circle the body of water that can have salt water or fresh water.

Page 53

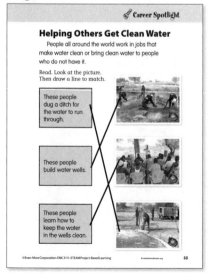

Helping Others Get Clean Water

People all around the world work in jobs that make water clean or bring clean water to people who do not have it.

Read. Look at the picture. Then draw a line to match.

These people dug a ditch for the water to run through.

These people build water wells.

These people learn how to keep the water in the wells clean.

Page 67

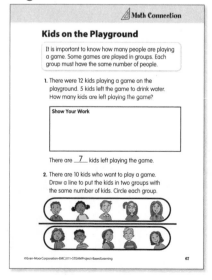

Kids on the Playground

It is important to know how many people are playing a game. Some games are played in groups. Each group must have the same number of people.

1. There were 12 kids playing a game on the playground. 5 kids left the game to drink water. How many kids are left playing the game?

   Show Your Work

   There are 7 kids left playing the game.

2. There are 10 kids who want to play a game. Draw a line to put the kids in two groups with the same number of kids. Circle each group.

Page 68

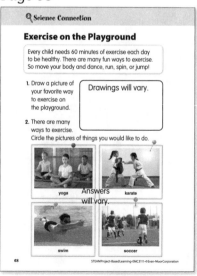

Exercise on the Playground

Every child needs 60 minutes of exercise each day to be healthy. There are many fun ways to exercise. So move your body and dance, run, spin, or jump!

1. Draw a picture of your favorite way to exercise on the playground.
   Drawings will vary.

2. There are many ways to exercise. Circle the pictures of things you would like to do.

   yoga   karate
   Answers will vary.
   swim   soccer

126

Page 69

Page 83

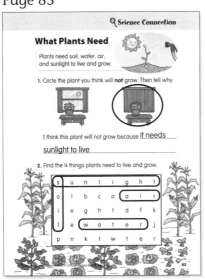

Page 84

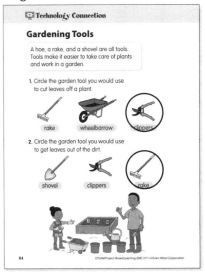

Page 85

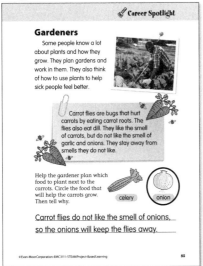

Page 99

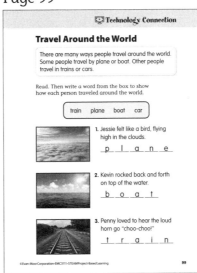

Page 100

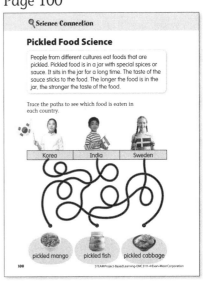

Page 115

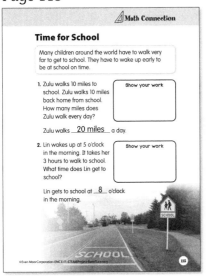

Page 117

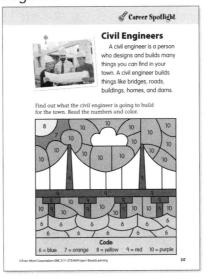